WORDS OF POWER

TRANSFORM YOUR LIFE
THE ART OF MANIFESTATION

Marion Weinstein

Earth Magic Productions, Inc.

Other Works by Marion Weinstein

Books

Positive Magic: Ancient Metaphysical Techniques For Modern Lives

Earth Magic: A Book Of Shadows For Positive Witches

Magic For Peace: A Nonsectarian Guide To Working Positive Magic For Peace And Safety

Marion Weinstein's Handy Guide To The I Ching

Marion Weinstein's Handy Guide To Tarot Cards

The Ancient/Modern Witch

CDs/Audiotapes

Personal Magic: The Role And The True Self, A Live Workshop

How To Read Tarot Cards, A Live Workshop

Marion Weinstein: Stand-Up Witch

How To Use The I Ching, A Live Workshop

Divination: Beyond Tea Leaves, A Live Workshop

How To Use Words Of Power, A Live Workshop

Magic For Peace: A Nonsecterian Guide To Working Positive Magic For Peace And Safety

The Ancient/Modern Witch

WORDS OF POWER

ISBN: 978-1-890733-18-6
© 2008
Edited And Typeset By Robert Blair & Sheila Galke
Cover Design By Sheila Galke
Printed in the U.S.A.

www.marionweinstein.com

This book, as all my work, is lovingly dedicated to my mother, Sylvia Linder Weinstein: Always an inspiration and always a help.

Acknowledgements

The author wishes to thank the following for their immeasurable contributions and help for this book:

Sheila Galke
Robert Blair
Alberta S. Libbey
Brian Klein
Donna Henes
Merlin Stone
The Goddess Isis

Contents

PART II
CHAPTER SEVEN

CHAPTER EIGHT

CHAPTER NINE

CHAPTER TEN

CHAPTER ELEVEN

CHAPTER TWELVE

AFTERWORD

PREFACE

In The Ancient World, magic was an integral part of daily life. And the origin of all magic was Egypt. The source of Egyptian Magic was found in The Mysteries of Isis.

All later mystical and occult traditions come from that one source—including alchemy, Ceremonial Magic, Jewish and Christian mysticism and Witchcraft (Wicca).

Words of Power come directly from Isis. Words of Power are an ancient technique to create and manifest essentially anything we want.

The main message Isis has to give us is to discover the Divinity within each one of us. Thus we transform our lives.

Δ⋆ Δ⋆ Δ⋆

The One Power
Working for through this book
Creates and manifests the work of Words Of Power
and the Magic of Isis
Into the lives of all who want it
According to free will
And for the good of all
And So Mote It Be!

FOREWORD

Words of Power are not meant to replace medical or psychiatric help. However, Words of Power Statements can help us to manifest the correct professional help we may seek.

Even if you do not wish to use Words of Power for actual manifestation in your life, you still may use the Statements to provide a positive focus for personal development. However, if you are looking for an effective technique to create manifestation and change, you have come to the right place!

With Words of Power, there is no need to give up any religion or belief. There is also no need to convert to any religion or belief.

Words of Power work well with many forms of prayer, although you may find yourself examining the meaning behind the way you have thought about prayer in the past. Words of Power do not reflect any particular religion.

With Words of Power, or any other system, I always say: mix and match and *create your own theology.*

INTRODUCTION

I wrote this book because it is the book I most wanted to read. Well, *somebody* had to write it! Words of Power are word sequences or verbal formulas. They change our lives and transform reality as we know it—in surprisingly practical and dramatic ways.

They are the great grandparents of prayer. They are similar to affirmations, Blessings, Wiccan spells, Buddhist chants, Western magical formulas and even many forms of Judeo-Christian prayer. But they are also different. Words of Power create *manifestations.* They literally make things happen.

The use of words to create actual change has led many people to believe that the power and the magic are in the words themselves. But this is an illusion.

Words of Power are an expression of a worldview, which outlines a specific relationship of the self to the rest of the Universe. This relationship is human to Divine, microcosm to Macrocosm, the sacred embodied in human form in relation to the sacred in its most vast form. Contrary to some practices, Words of Power emphasize and use your inherent divine power.

In researching Words of Power, I went all the way back to the work of the Goddess Isis in Ancient Egypt. Much of the information in this book was channelled. Isis was known to be able to do anything. She created miracles of healing, including bringing the dead back to life. Many of the ancient Egyptians worshipped Her as a Deity, but they really should have worshipped themselves—because She was trying to reveal to them their own personal power and teach them manifestation.

"Come to me, for my speech hath in it the power to protect, and it possesseth life... For I am Isis the Goddess, and I am the Lady of Words of Power, and I know how to work with Words of Power, and most mighty are my words!" [1]

Words Of Power Statement

Here is a sample 21st Century Words of Power Statement that you may use for yourself, based on the Principles taught by Isis.

Words of Power Statement for the Goal of Success

Generic Style:

1. There is One Power, which is The Universal Power

2. Which includes perfect success of every kind

3. And I, (your name here), am The Universal Power incarnate

4. Therefore, I create and manifest perfect success in my life here, now and always

5. According to free will

6. And for the good of all

7. I now release all cause, effect, manifestation, form and essence, belief or idea of anything less than complete success

8. I replace this with perfect success of every kind, here, now and always

9. And so this must be!

Part I of this book, which follows, gives the background and Principles for creating Words of Power with full understanding of the process. Part II will provide sample Words of Power Statements and all the components you need to create Statements for a large variety of goals. Each Statement varies according to your Deity or Power Source, goal and finale style. Words of Power Statements may be said out loud or silently, alone, with a partner, or in a group.

The last few pages of this book provide both blank outlines for you to create your own Words of Power Statements, as well as some complete Statements for our planet earth.

Personalized Interactive Words Of Power Statements can be found at www.marionweinstein.com.

PART I

CHAPTER ONE

THE IMPORTANCE OF OUR WORLDVIEW

There are many different ways of looking at our lives and the rest of the Universe. We all have ways that make us comfortable.

We may not always be satisfied, but most of us have worked out some sort of worldview—and system for expressing it. Our worldview makes sense and feels comfortable, telling us, "This is the way things work:"

- Family is over here.

- Death is over there.

- God (or religion) is over here.

- Science (and medicine) tells us...

- Money is: hard to get, the root of all evil, controlled by the government or establishment, something to work for or toward...

- Luck is...

- Love is...

- War is...

- Weight is...

- Youth is...

(Fill in the details for yourself.)

Lenny Bruce said that we are still mentally living in communal caves—with areas put aside for eating meals, to use as a bathroom, to worship, sleep or have sex. If anyone used an area in the cave incorrectly, the entire tribe would turn on him or her—because they would no longer feel *comfortable.* Life is difficult enough and scary enough with dinosaurs stomping around outside, without someone destroying our comfort zone, the one place we feel safe—our cave.

Yet sometimes the comfort zone no longer provides enough answers for everything we may encounter in life. Then, people will flock to the latest self-help expert, or the nearest storefront gypsy (often not much of a difference), or the nearest spaceship or comet. We may explore psychology or science or religion—or various religions—and then we may add or subtract some more details to our worldview and to our system for dealing with our lives.

THE NEED FOR CHANGE

At different times in our lives, we may find ourselves really wanting to make changes. We may feel this need in varying degrees of desperation and explore different ways to make change happen. People may turn to drugs, to gurus, to cults or simply to new relationships. Sometimes people try to leave this life altogether. Some succeed, and sometimes, especially with celebrities, this may seem to be accidental.

But even for more "everyday" people, we may feel dissatisfaction with our lives in various ways. There is nothing wrong with feeling this. In fact, it often takes courage to face. If there is anything in your own life that you are not happy about—whether it is a large circumstance or a small one—please allow yourself to accept that this is a valid feeling.

Sometimes we may be unhappy about feeling that we cannot actually change anything. But we can. There are numerous techniques to create change in our lives. I have been researching this subject for most of my life. And now I am happy to share with you my favorite technique: Words of Power.

⏃⏃⏃

CHAPTER TWO

It's astonishing to me that the technique of Words of Power is not a prominent part of our culture. For many years, metaphysical and magical techniques used to be secret. People were illiterate, generally ignorant and perhaps not considered to be "ready" to acknowledge their own personal power—at least in the eyes of the establishment, government or church. Now we live in a culture that's widely literate, most people are relatively intelligent and yet this particular technique, this way of dealing with the world, is still barely known. It's far from common knowledge, not valued, and too often misunderstood. However, it is coming back in surprising ways.

When I wrote my first book, *Positive Magic*—which I still consider to be my life's work—I wrote one long chapter, *Words of Power, Chapter Eight.* It took me an entire year to write it. That was thirty years ago. Words of Power are now creeping back into our culture, often known as *affirmations.* They create transformation and can dramatically change your personal reality, all accomplished with words. The difference between affirmations and Words of Power is: Words of Power always draw upon your divine personal Power Source.

To this day, every time I think about Words of Power, give a talk, write about it, or practice it myself—which is often—I have a deepening understanding. So I realize it's not a subject you can just immediately learn in its entirety; I know I couldn't. But I can pretty much guarantee that the more you practice it, the more you think about it and the more you learn peripheral information about it, the better you'll understand how it works, and the more effective your work will be. A basic understanding, as provided here, is an excellent beginning, which is enough to start doing some effective manifestation work right away.

CREATING CHANGE

The core idea is that *you can create anything.*

This may be hard to believe, and yet the more you believe it, the more it will be true for you.

First, I will give you the Principles on which this work is based. Next, we will actually do the work of Words of Power, specifically and carefully for ourselves. We will explore the different styles you can choose, to see which resonates most deeply for you.

MAGIC, THE WORLD OF FORM AND THE INVISIBLE WORLD

The work of magic (Positive Magic, of course) may be defined as *transformation.* This usually refers to transforming the World of Form in which we live—the visible, touch-able world, as we know it. But transformation of the Invisible World takes place as well, because these two Worlds coexist. I often refer to the Invisible World as "The Invisible Realm," because by its very nature, it doesn't have parameters.

WHAT IS REALITY?

All of so-called reality is subject to change at a moment's notice. This is a concept that may seem amazing at first. The points to remember are:

1. *Perception creates reality.* Reality is based on our perception. You can change your perception, and thus you can change your reality. Now, some people can do this simply with thoughts. Well, we actually all can, and we all actually do this automatically, to some extent. But if you change your reality *with words,* you will be extremely clear, specific and in control. Your words in turn then change your thoughts!

2. *Your worldview determines your perception.* Our culture has in a large part influenced and determined our worldview, for each one of us. When we do the work of Words of Power, we are really making a choice to step outside of our culture and take a larger worldview.

3. *Your worldview determines your ability to access your personal power.* When we expand our worldview, we automatically increase our personal power.

THE MOVIE CAMERA METHOD

To help us expand our worldview, I like to use the analogy of filming a movie:

First, there's the *close-up,* which shows the individual's face. Then there's the *two-shot,* viewed from a little further back and generally showing two people. Then there's the *long shot,* which shows more aspects of the picture, including background. Next, as the camera pulls further back, there's the *crane shot,* which is a wide view as seen from above. And finally, there is the *helicopter shot,* which is taken from an even higher and broader vantage point and shows even more of the scene than any other shot. This is a good foundation for the work of Words of Power—a helicopter shot of reality. This provides a far larger view than the current culture's worldview. The original view still exists, but now we see all possibilities along with that original view, changing our perception. The larger view contains the basic idea that *perception creates reality.* A smaller view makes it seem as though reality is somehow a simple fact that has nothing to do with perception at all.

So we all have been limited in the way we perceive reality, and consequently we all have felt limited in our personal power. But that feeling of limitation is only *perception.*

This work has in the past been categorized as "occult" or "magic." Anyway, definitions are choices, just as what we call reality is also a choice. Now, this work is called *metaphysics,* which means "beyond physics" or "greater than physics."

Religious Science, Christian Science and other "modern" religions may define themselves as not only metaphysical religions, but also somehow forms of science. However, they still work with one principal Deity, (male) God—so they still come from a patriarchal monotheistic vantage point. I do not mean to say in any sense that this is bad. These religions depart from traditional Judeo-Christian religion in that they use *affirmations,* and in so doing they bridge a certain gap between affirmation and traditional prayer.

Another departure from traditional Western religious thought in these "metaphysical" religions is the belief that the World of Form (popularly considered to be "reality") contains *visible manifestations of invisible ideas.* In this context, we too are considered to be visible, physical manifestations of invisible ideas. In other words, we are *ideas in form.* Our bodies are seen as physical expressions of our ideas and thoughts. We are defined as spiritual beings in physical form.

All of this is similar to Positive Magic, until we get to the basis of these religions' Power Source, which is still patriarchal and monotheistic—which I personally find limiting, although I do respect it. Here is another part I agree with: These religions teach that when you change an (invisible) idea, you change the corresponding *form,* and thus you change your life. So we can say that when we change an idea about ourselves on the invisible level, we consequently change our lives on the physical level as well. This concept is in large part the way that healing works.

CHAPTER THREE

THE KABBALAH

The Kabbalah is a Hebrew mystery school started in early Jewish culture, which flourished in the 17th Century, and still exists today, although it has changed greatly in its current popular Hollywood form. The Kabbalah has also branched into a Christian version. In Hebrew, the Kabbalistic word for the Earth Plane is called *Malkuth.*

מלכות

The Kabbalah acknowledges that the Earth Plane is a quite limited place compared to the vast Invisible area, with which it co-exists. Holy people have traditionally made miracles manifest on the Earth Plane. Adepts, Magicians, Sorcerers, Wizards, Wonder Rabbis, Shamans and magical priests of every culture (usually male) traditionally worked their magic in the Invisible Realm. Then, when the goal manifested in the visible world, people who were onlookers, who didn't understand the process, would think that such work is solely accomplished on the physical, Earth Plane, because this seems to be the most obvious explanation. But the actual work includes both Worlds—as it will for us.

I have chosen the use of words as the best way to accomplish transformation and manifestation. Yes, we could use chants, music or rituals, which enact the process in microcosm. We could also use meditation or visualization. These are all becoming popular ways to work. But even with any or all of these techniques, I still believe we should also use words. We can control the situation in more detail with words. Words provide a familiar, accessible bridge to the power of the Invisible Realm.

LANGUAGE

I also say we should use words in the language which we speak, the language that is clearest to us. Words are symbols and they have power whether they are written or spoken. There is a tradition of using "magical languages," such as Hebrew, Latin, Egyptian and Ancient Greek; these are actually very old languages. Magic has traditionally been worked in such languages, because they were the vernacular of the people doing the magic at that time. For us to work magic in these languages—even though this may seem very mystical and almost theatrical—doesn't really make sense. We should always work magic in the language that makes the most sense to us, that we understand the best. There are many stories of people chanting or repeating phrases when they didn't know what they were talking about, or reading passages from a dusty old "grimoire" or magic text. Dangerous episodes invariably took place: apparitions, negative entities and demonic beings appeared (at least in movies). For now, let us just say: *speak in the language you understand best.* Always try to strip away the mystery.

CHAPTER FOUR

HOW WORDS OF POWER STATEMENTS WORK: THE THREEFOLD LAW

This is actually the only law in Witchcraft (Wicca), and it is very simple: *Everything you do comes back to you three times.* Does this happen exactly three times? Does it happen more than three times? Perhaps three times is a good metaphor because it explains how magic works: Here we are in the Visible World (the World of Form); actually, we're in both Worlds simultaneously, but we tend to focus on the Visible World first.

1. So, we do the work in this World of Form, say our Words of Power here, perhaps with an accompanying ritual but not necessarily so.

2. Next, our words go out into the Invisible Realm which includes all time and all space.

3. And then when the magic manifests back in this Visible World, we readily see its result in Form. Thus, magic works in three steps.

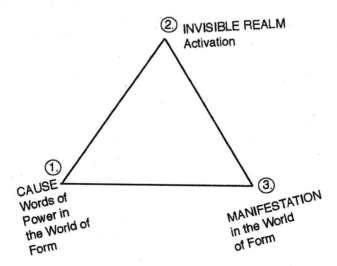

Actually, the process of manifestation is taking place in all time and all space, anyway. When we direct our manifestation in a conscious, purposeful way, the very process of doing so serves to constantly empower ourselves. Clear language—the language we understand—helps in accessing our personal power.

Many religions have had built-in systems which serve to enforce the illusion that people have little or no personal power. Consequently, people who believe they don't have personal power do not have it to use. An analogy: you could have the most effective electrical system in your house, but if you don't realize that you have it, you won't turn on the switch. So it is with personal power—if you don't know that you have it, you won't have it to use. Once you simply get the information that you do have it, such awareness makes an excellent starting point for
using it.

An awareness of personal power is not the same as over-compensation. Overcompensation is a belief in possessing unusual superpower and this is an expression of personal feelings of inherent weakness. This feeds impulses from the ego, not your divine Power Source. The constant goal with Words of Power is total satisfaction—not compromise, not rationalization and not over-compensation.

PERSONAL POWER

I believe that *the medium is the message.* When Marshal Mcluhan made this famous statement, he was referring to electronic media: television and radio. But I always believed the application could be carried much further— in this case, into religion. The medium is the message often, in many forms of prayer and also in any magical work that has built into it the idea of *giving away personal power.* If we give away our personal power at the start, by blindly following somebody else's instructions or beliefs, it can automatically limit the effects of manifestation. Cultural beliefs can create a limiting influence, as they contribute to establishing a limited worldview. Such a limitation may seem valid to us.

We can begin by noticing and overcoming cultural limitations intellectually, even before we may respond emotionally. Yet in order to do this work in its most powerful form, it is crucial to position yourself correctly in relation to the Universal Power Source. Even choosing a name for this can be a pitfall. By saying, "God, Goddess or Deity," one has to be infinitely watchful that one isn't inadvertently lapsing into a traditional limiting definition. Often some names may have limiting connotations from the past. If so, one could give away at least part of one's personal power at the very start—completely unaware that one is doing so. When choosing your Deity, open your mind completely, say each name aloud and use one that seems to awaken a meaningful power or presence within you.

Differences Between Prayer And Words Of Power

These are the differences between supplication (prayer) and affirmations (Words of Power). There is an area of so-called "modern prayer," in which people endeavor to pray out of an enlightened philosophical state, or to deal with the concept of a traditional God in a "modern" way as an equal, or theological partner. Nonetheless, this still qualifies as supplication—which is not necessarily bad in any way. It is just a state of mind that I view as limited. However, if one does take that stance in relation to Deity, I would recommend to at least be aware of doing so.

Amongst truly thoughtful holy people in various religions, it is understood that God is not a literally anthropomorphized superman with a beard and a robe, sitting on a throne and able to grant our wishes. But many people are still projecting some image of that Deity, which they learned as children—even if they claim to have rejected it. Supplication takes various forms, but usually involves *diminishing the perception of the self.* This is usually accomplished either by bowing down—even just symbolically bowing the head—kneeling, clasping the hands. The more spiritual

goal of these traditional practices is to help diminish the false ego
self and connect to one's inner Deity. However the traditional be-
haviors can go too far: sometimes even completely lying face down
on the ground, prostrate, groveling. There were various medieval
masochistic activities, in which people actually hit themselves, and
whipped their flesh with special implements, causing terrible pain
and drawing blood. Whatever the psychopathology involved, the
religious goal was to perceive themselves *as less than* their Deity.

In traditional prayer, we find the widespread belief that the
Deity is in heaven, and is male, and the human self is on Earth and
is puny. The vision of the self as child-like and the Deity as a parent, has affected all of our culture. I'm not saying this is bad—or
good—I'm just pointing to the psychological result, the reflection
of this vision throughout our culture: Our culture is hierarchal, our
government still male-dominated, women and children are not re-
spected or treated as equally as men. In many cultures, such as the
Middle East, women have been devalued, their activities limited,
and their punishment barbaric to a dangerous degree. This all re-
flects the society's vision of a superior male Deity.

The very structure of many prayers—no matter how poetic
or inspiring—evokes supplication and automatically positions the
human self as beneath the Universal Power Source—for most
people.

In contrast, Words of Power provide a way of establishing
one's link to the Universal Power Source and confirming one's right
and ability to use it. I believe that spiritually advanced or "holy" people have always known about this important point and have in fact
been trying to teach ordinary people for centuries, for eons, how
to work affirmation. But it seems that anytime a holy person has
tried to teach the concept of personal power—the holy person invariably ended up being worshiped. And all too often, as we have
seen with various gurus in our own culture, certain erstwhile holy
people have not been able to resist buying themselves a few Rolls
Royces and expensive jewels, because of the temptation provided

by being worshipped! People tend to give their all-too-human gurus money, cars and sex—until goodbye, spirituality. Not always, of course. But these are some of the pitfalls that come along with believing that someone possesses *exclusive* spiritual knowledge. In contrast, Words of Power are for everybody and are based on the premise that we all have equal personal divine power. Therefore, we don't have to convince anyone to give us anything, because we all can give to ourselves whatever we like.

$$\Delta^{\star}_{\cong} \quad \Delta^{\star}_{\cong} \quad \Delta^{\star}_{\cong}$$

CHAPTER FIVE

CARGO CULTS

During World War II, and shortly after, in some remote regions—Pacific islands and jungles—when a plane would arrive with cargo such as radios, food, beads, flashlights, whatever, people who had never seen a plane before would worship *the plane.* Sometimes they even built a whole religion around the plane after it left, waiting for it to come back. Some built primitive airplane-like structures, which didn't do anything except superficially look like planes. Some worshiped the pilots, and have legends about them even generations later. I sometimes wonder: Is our entire planet a cargo cult? Are we waiting for some extra-terrestrial pilots to return?[2] During the '70s and '80s this was a popular theory dubbed "Ancient Astronauts." The theory here is that many early legends in various cultures including ours, could be referring—through the eyes of primitive people—to heavenly beings who either ascended to Heaven (as in Jacob's Ladder) or came down to Earth (such as the angels who announced the birth of Jesus).

HISTORY OF WORDS OF POWER

This work has many titles besides affirmation. In some metaphysical religions it is called "treatment," in some magical traditions it is known as blessing, magic spells, enchantments and, of course, prayer. Although there are many names for this work, and many groups claim ownership of it, I believe it was originally taught in Ancient Egyptian and Greek Mystery Schools, including the Eleusinian Mysteries. The New Testament also refers to the power of words.

"In the beginning was the word and the word was with God and the word was God."[3] There are clues that it was known to Moses of the Old Testament. He studied in Egypt.

"Moses was educated in all the learning of the Egyptians, and he was a man of power in words and deeds."[4] This might explain the apparent magic that Moses demonstrated.

The ancient Chinese oracle, The *I Ching*, refers to the power of words, dating back over 4000 years.

"Heat creates energy: this is signified by the wind stirred up by the fire and issuing forth from it. This represents influence working from within outward... In order to be capable of producing such an influence, one's words must have power, and this they can have only if they are based on something real, just as flame depends on its fuel."[5]

SUPERSTITION AND FEAR

The idea of words having power is found in every culture. Sometimes superstition is involved. Superstition is based on fear—which, of course, has always been a normal reaction to the harsher side of life; but it can be overcome. Fear must be acknowledged and faced, and essentially stripped of all negative power. In Words of Power, we do this with the Release Statement.

Fear can be tricky, especially if it is hidden. Years ago I was giving a lecture on Witchcraft in East Hampton, to a crowd of resident writers and intellectuals. Afterward, a couple approached me, dressed obviously like Witches. They were wearing black from head to toe, with lots of silver and crystal Witchcraft jewelry; he had a beard and she had a silver crown-like ornament on her head. They were clearly proud of looking so very Witch-like. But they both looked intensely worried; they asked me in whispered tones if I was ever afraid that "God would be angry" at what I'm doing. I told them about the helicopter shot idea mentioned earlier, that as Witches we can go up *beyond* where the belief in an angry, judgmental God seems valid, and see that the belief in such a Deity is part of a much larger picture. This is not to say that such a version of God does not exist or that it is a bad concept, just that the belief structure surrounding such a Deity is a choice—one among many. This particular familiar version of Deity, as punishing/rewarding, is fear-based, and also establishes the idea that God is thoroughly mysterious. In the Jewish Kabbalah, God's very name is secret, and being able to pronounce it is not allowed nor even considered to be possible. His ways are unknowable; they cannot be predicted or understood. And somehow finding out the secret name is believed to be a source of great mystical power and the ability to create miracles.

In the work of Words of Power, we could say that the secret name is this: *We ourselves are each what is known as "God."* We each are defined as that theological entity. This is not just a little semantic trick. If you say the name, you are claiming it as yours—and you have to understand its hidden meaning on a deeper and deeper level. And I think the very best way to understand it is to use a word sequence such as the one we consistently use in Words of Power.

$$\Delta^\star_\ominus \quad \Delta^\star_\ominus \quad \Delta^\star_\ominus$$

CHAPTER SIX

WORD POWER

I cannot emphasize enough how important it is to understand everything that we do and say, and to watch our words. Our culture is learning the importance of this principle. A good example is the way that new, politically correct definitions of people are reframing previously negative conditions. For example, instead of saying somebody is "crippled," "handicapped" or "disabled" we now say, "physically challenged." This is an empowering use of words that's entirely new. More and more people are spontaneously choosing to redefine such a situation as inherently positive.

MA'KHERU, THE WORD OF TRUTH

The theory and belief behind Ma'Kheru is simply this: *every word you say comes true.* This can be automatic, as it often is in daily life, or accomplished with the work of Words of Power or some other technique. The idea is that when we say something, we are actually *creating* whatever we are saying. So, for example, if people continually say that they're sick, then eventually they very well may become physically sick. Also, if they believe other people saying there is something wrong with them, they very well may take in, actually embody (create) whatever the other says is wrong. That's why early childhood influences are so important. They help to create the child's reality throughout life.

I have become so careful about what I say (and write) that I no longer even say that something negative is actually a fact. I *qualify* my statements, such as " this seems to be..." and I recommend this watchfulness all the time. The point is simply to *watch your words.* Yes, even if you are not actually working with Words of Power, even when you're "off duty," do learn to be super-aware of all of your words, both spoken and written. This may take some time until it becomes automatic, but it is well worth the effort.

So, even if you work with Words of Power every day, and successfully change your life for the better in many ways—if one day you happen to go shopping and say, "You don't have any lettuce, do you?" You might actually create a situation in which the store will be out of lettuce! And if you say instead, "I'm sure you have some really good lettuce," guess what you'll find? This may seem to be a really simple or small example, but it's infinitely meaningful in its applications.

The connotations of the principle of Ma'Kheru are vast: *every word you say comes true, anyway,* whether you want it to or not. Next, the goal is to get to the point where your words are so carefully framed that you automatically make everything you say come true.

$$\Delta^{\star}_{\circ} \quad \Delta^{\star}_{\circ} \quad \Delta^{\star}_{\circ}$$

PART II

CHAPTER SEVEN

THE PRINCIPLES OF WORDS OF POWER

1. THE INFINITY OF SOLUTION

It is important to clear out limited, conditional ideas in order to get to the starting point for manifestation. The starting point for Words of Power is: *Anything is possible.* This starting point is also part of whatever goal we work for. The Infinity of Solution simply means that there are always an infinite number of possibilities, of answers and solutions to any situation. These exist far beyond any possibilities our minds may have yet conceived. After all, scientists agree that we use only one fraction of our brains. This is true for everyone, even so-called experts. Maybe there are solutions *no one* has thought of yet! By being open to the Infinity of Solution, we allow literally any solution to take place. Yes, even one that may seem like a miracle.

2. NON-MANIPULATION

Always harm no one, and help all. At first, this concept may seem difficult to understand in our current culture which seems to believe that there always have to be winners and losers in every situation. But let's at least accept intellectually—even as a possibility—that there don't have to be winners or losers and that we can harm no one and help all. Eventually, this idea will become clear as when we work Words of Power, we consistently say:

"According to free will,
And for the good of all."

Many people still misunderstand magic, thinking that it is all about "making" someone do something (or not do something). This is really a limited view and it's certainly not true of Positive Magic. Accordingly, with Words of Power, we do not use other people's names.

3. FORM AND ESSENCE

When choosing a goal, it is better to work for a general result (essence) rather than any detail (form), or even a whole list of details. As a general rule: when you use words, essence turns out to be actually more satisfying than any form.

EQOB:[6] This is a shortcut term for the concept, "This, its equivalent or better." Even when working for a form as a goal, it's important to bear in mind that the form could turn out to be totally different and still be appropriate, or even better. Saying "EQOB" allows you to name the form, without being limited to it.

4. THE LAW OF CAUSE AND EFFECT

This is a basic law of physics. As applied to our personal lives, everything we do, say or even think, is a cause, and has an effect. In daily life, we are constantly creating causes—or somehow allowing them to happen—and we are just as constantly experiencing the effects. For example, if we go out into the rain without an umbrella or a raincoat, that is a cause—and the effect would be getting wet. Ideally, we strive for awareness to choose and plan the cause carefully (a metaphysical umbrella and raincoat, we could say)—so that we control the effect. The Words of Power we say provide the cause. The goal(s) for which we work are the effect(s).

5. POWER SOURCE

Some people consider this a religious idea. Human beings all over our world have developed many names, visions and concepts for The Universal Power Source: Deity, Goddess, God, Spirit, Jesus, Holy Spirit, The Creator, The Force, Creatrix, Higher Power, The Man Upstairs, The Woman Upstairs, etc. Unfortunately, and ironically, these definitions of our Power Source, particularly the word "God," have too often led to just the opposite of their originally beneficent intentions. Instead of love and harmony, people have invoked prejudice and war. With Words of Power, as in prayer, it is infinitely important to spend time and thought over the concept of who and what your Power Source is, and what it stands for. *What is most sacred to you?* Whom do you believe in, or What do you believe in, and how do you relate to Him, Her or It? Perhaps instead of a specific religious name, you choose Nature, Science or Reason. Whatever you choose—this choice is the source of your personal power, so please think carefully and choose with all your heart, mind and soul. We each have a personal relationship to—and alignment with—our Power Source. It ideally contains all that is most sacred to us. We perceive ourselves to be part of this source, and we activate this alignment. According to the philosophy with which I work, the ideal form of this alignment is:

We are each a perfect manifestation of the Universal Power Source, or

We are each God, Goddess or Deity incarnate (in human form, on Earth).

If this wording suits you—of course please use it. However, since this part of the work is so personal, you may change the wording to express your deepest beliefs.

If you choose a Deity, think of the best your Deity has to offer—the highest principles—and define that for yourself, and choose to work with that. A list of international Deities is coming up.

6. EQUAL PERSONAL POWER

Everyone has equal—or potentially equal—personal power from the Power Source.

This is the reason we don't need any special power or middleman (or middlewoman) to work Words of Power for us.

All we have to do is activate the personal power that we each already have, and to do this responsibly, According to Free Will and For The Good of All.

7. WE ARE ALL LINKED

Another way of stating this Principle is: *The Oneness of All Life.* This is a clear concept, which speaks for itself. It also explains how working for our own highest good is automatically for the good of all, including beings anywhere on Earth and beyond.

8. ALL TIME AND ALL SPACE

When we work Words of Power, when we pray or when we use any form of Positive Magic, we are not limited by time and space, as we know it. The relatively new field of Quantum Physics also delineates the concept of limitless time and space. Our work takes place in All Time and All Space. This is really ancient information that holy people in most religions have known about and used for centuries.

9. PERSONAL RESPONSIBILITY; NO GUILT AND NO BLAME

When we embark upon the work of transformation and manifestation, it is important to take responsibility, without guilt or blame, for all of our own actions and even thoughts. Doing this frees our personal energy and power. Taking personal responsibility clarifies the process: "I created this situation, and now I can change it to a situation more clearly of my own choosing. I release the former situation, and create the new one which I now want."

1O. Perception Creates Reality

Let us re-visit this philosophical idea. It can be understood on many levels. Various self-help courses are based on this Principle. For the purposes of this work, let us simply repeat: *We each have the power to create our world and change our lives.*

We do this by carefully observing what we perceive, see and consequently believe. Working with Words of Power is a way of controlling and directing this process. Even without specifically working with Words of Power—This Principle still holds true: If we change our beliefs, we automatically create change in our lives. Remember that The Law of Cause and Effect is constantly going on, not only in Words of Power, but also in daily life. This is also true of perception creating reality—it is an ongoing process.

In addition:
- If we believe in something, this can help make it happen.

- If we fear something, this can also help make it happen (unintentionally)—by means of our heightened focus.

- Negative thoughts and ideas can make negative things manifest.

- Positive thoughts and ideas can make positive things manifest.

CHAPTER EIGHT

DEALING WITH NEGATIVES

I think it is unrealistic to expect ourselves to immediately get rid of all negative feelings and thoughts, such as anger, fear or discouragement. If we expect ourselves to do this, we might simply deny negatives. Denial certainly does not make them disappear; it hides them. But they must be dealt with. Thoughts and words can create negative effects—whether we deny them or not. This is true in all areas of daily life.

INSTANT TRANSFORMATION

Here is what I believe to be the single most effective "clean up" technique.

Strip the negative idea, thought, feeling or statement— whatever it is—of all negative or harmful power. One quick method is to say "I take it out of the Law" (meaning The Law of Cause and Effect). Or say, "No harmful power; turn this to good." This way, the negative will not become a cause for further problems, and it is also immediately transformed into something life-affirming and positive. If it's too embarrassing or inappropriate to say any of this out loud, just silently think it. Remember, even when you are "off duty"—not doing Words of Power—your words, thoughts and images still have power. So pay attention to what you say, feel or visualize. Try not to say things like "This is terrible," or "That is going to be a disaster," etc. Try instead to make this kind of adjustment: "This *seems* terrible," or "That *looks* like a disaster, but maybe not..." And if you ever find yourself picturing unpleasant or even terrible things—stop the mental picture. Run your mental videotape back—and then play it again in your head, this time showing positive, *life-affirming* images of the same subject. In this way, without denying your true concerns, you can still avoid puttingnegative images onto the Law of Cause and Effect. Instead, you are actually ritually correcting the situation.

When working with Words of Power, try to notice how you are feeling at the time. If you recognize any negative feelings, carefully take them out of your work and out of the Law of Cause and Effect. You may do this verbally: As release work, take out fear, worry, anger, hate—all of that. It's certainly understandable to feel these things, and important not to deny them. But they could limit your effectiveness and cause problems. Acknowledge, release and replace them. I recommend this sequence:

1. Release any negative, and

2. Replace it with its positive opposite. For example, release anger and replace it with constructive energy.

3. You could also replace a negative with The Infinity of Solution.

It's always important to replace something you have released with something else. Never leave any metaphysical "holes."

Watching one's words, thoughts, feelings, ideas and images in this way may seem excessive, but doing so will become second nature after awhile. Not only will your Words of Power work be more accurate and successful, but you'll also feel more optimistic and be more in control of your life.

What if someone else seems to be setting up negative causes and effects? Certainly if anyone is talking about you, you can (usually silently) release and take it out, say "no harmful power; turn it to good." If the person is talking about another or others, or predicting bad things for a group or for the world in general—also take out such a prediction, release it, strip it of all negative or harmful power, and turn it to good.

Acting In Accordance

Working with Words of Power is not intended to be *instead of action;* it is always used *along with* appropriate action. When we work Words of Power for a specific goal—for example, abundance—we may follow up by actively pursuing work projects, job interviews, investment inquiries and/or anything else that we belive will help manifest abundance. Also, in our lives, there is actual power in the way we behave. You could say that the way we live our lives sets off vibrations. If we all try to act peacefully and not angrily or negatively in daily life, this will actually create a powerful vibration of peace in the atmosphere of our world.

Chapter Nine

The Work Of Manifestation

1. The Law Of Attraction And Affinity Manifestation

Essentially, this cosmic legislation states that *like attracts like;* that one can *draw* to oneself whatever one needs or wants, if one uses this law "creatively." The belief here is that everything exists (in potential, at least) *somewhere* in the Universe, and all one needs to do is name and/or visualize that which one needs or wants, and affirm that one can and will get it. The goal might be a material object, or it might be an intangible state, such as health or love. In doing so, one will draw the goal to oneself.

Any form of manifestation work which is based on this Law, is *Affinity Manifestation.* But many other techniques, which might not specifically mention the Law of Attraction, still fall into this category; that is, if such techniques are based upon a belief that manifestation is brought about by a process of consciously *drawing to you* that which is your goal. This idea in itself is revolutionary to many people, and it has provided a positive force for good, which is not to be minimized.

However, in my experience, Affinity Manifestation has one major drawback: If you believe that somewhere out in the Universe there exists that which you need or want, and you must now do specific work to draw it to you—then you might possibly lapse into sensing a feeling of *distance* between your current situation and that which you want to achieve. You might experience feelings of intense need or lack. You might feel an awareness that now, even as you do this work, you do not yet have this "thing," this goal, or whatever the end result is which you want. You may feel, "It's not here yet. It's still out there." And attached to this feeling might be, "I can't help feeling terrible that it's not here yet!" Or even, "Maybe it will never be here."

I am concerned that this perception of lack that one might feel *while doing the work,* might go right into the work, and create a cause. Such perception of lack could manifest right along with the goal—as unwanted effects such as delay or dissatisfaction. So the very fact of focusing on the current state of *not-having* could perpetuate that very state. Even if you don't actually say, "I feel a sense of distance from my goal," the pain of feeling that distance (or even a related mild discomfort) might also go into the work, and consequently into the results. This can be very difficult to avoid. I have experienced it many times.

Before I learned about Creation Manifestation, the antidote I always used was this: I would work Words of Power to release the pain, the doubt, the perception of distance, or whatever that discomfort felt like—if I even recognized it. Then I would replace that with confidence, The Infinity of Solution, and any other positive ideas that seemed appropriate. This technique is completely effective, and I still recommend it.

However, a problem here could be that one might not notice certain feelings of doubt or lack. These feelings can be insidiously subtle and difficult to watch out for, because of their elusive nature and the state of mild depression and discouragement they can induce. In other words, a feeling of lack could sneak into the Words of Power, unnoticed, and one might not recognize the necessity to include the antidote work. Too often, unusual delays in manifestation can be traced to this very cause. You may well ask, *How can such timing be measured?* Also, *What's an appropriate pace for manifestation, anyway?* I would say, if one feels a true sense of dissatisfaction in one's own personal growth and life development, this might be evidence of unreasonable delay in manifestation. The ideal rate of growth, in my opinion, just feels right. This is purely a matter of perception, so only you will know. No one can ever possibly tell you what your rate of development "should" be. Various recent philosophies and books advocate affinity manifestation, even if they do not call it that. If you have diagnosed your work up until now as Affinity Manifestation, and wish instead to use Creation Manifestation, what is required first is a conceptual shift. Creation Manifestation begins with a different mindset than Affinity Manifestation.

2. CREATION MANIFESTATION

This is an expression of a truly holistic view of the Universe. At this level of work, the Oneness of all of Creation is affirmed. There is no separation. We are all linked; all is connected. Thus there is no separation between you and your goal. You are Goddess, you are God. You create. *You do not draw your goal to you, because it is not separate from you.* You manifest yourself *as that goal;* you create it.

CREATION STARTS WITH PERCEPTION

This is how the process works: First of all, there is no massive ego misunderstanding ("Hey, look at me, I'm a powerful God Incarnate!") because every living being is capable of working at this level. In fact, every being does work at this level, but not necessarily with the awareness that this is what we are all doing.
We may now direct our awareness in three ways:

1. We acknowledge that the process of *directed perception* is a means to creation.

2. We consciously choose to direct our perception in a specific way.

3. The way we do this is *to identify ourselves as the very goal for which we are working.*

Let's look at step 3 further.

WE BECOME THE GOAL WE ARE WORKING FOR

In fact, we acknowledge that we already *are* the goal we are working for. We now focus on *being* that goal. Does this mean that we are no longer ourselves, that we have somehow become the goal instead? Not at all. We are ourselves plus the goal.

In some competitions such as tennis and golf, the latest technique some players use to vastly improve their game is a sporty version of Zen meditation. The idea is that instead of focusing on their intense desire to hit the ball, they focus instead on the ball itself. They focus, in fact, on "being" the ball. In their mind's eye, *they become the ball.* Thus, they free themselves from trying to hit the ball, trying so hard that they actually can no longer hit it. And once they stop trying, that's when they hit the ball!

The idea is that when one tries too hard, one might not be able to accomplish something which one is perfectly capable of doing. Trying is what gets in the way. Instead of trying, the process of *becoming the goal* (in this case, the ball) releases the self from getting bogged down in trying too hard. Now the self is free to do what it has been capable of doing all along. In sports, that is hitting the ball. In our case, it is achieving any goal we choose in the most effective and transforming way.

In other words, we are creating that which we want—our goal—rather than drawing it to us. So we have decided to become that "thing" we want, that goal, whatever it is—in our minds.

WITH THE MIND'S EYE

It is often helpful to visualize our goal. Artists all know how to do this. As the saying goes, any work of art, before it is painted or sculpted, is first seen "with the mind's eye." Manifestation is definitely an art. So we are now all artists, and we may all look at our goals with our minds' eyes. But we do not force the image, nor do we manipulate it; we *allow* it to emerge. We may find that we are given spontaneous psychic pictures to help us do this.

HOW CREATION MANIFESTATION WORKS

1. Just to be able to see a goal, just to allow it to emerge in your mind's eye, is to perceive it.

2. And to perceive your goal is to create it.

3. If an image is in your mind, and your mind's eye is looking at it, then that image is by definition *part of you.*

4. If it is part of you, and you allow yourself to identify with it, you have, in effect "become" it. You have created it, and you have manifested it.

When you understand how this has happened, then the Words of Power, which you say to make your goal manifest visibly and tangibly—the same Words of Power which you may have said before—have subtly changed. They are now working at a different level, because your awareness is at a different level. In other words, your words have been *attracting* before, and now they are *creating.*

So, the important thing about working at this level is to be aware of how the process works. It is not necessary to state Words of Power very differently; you may simply acknowledge this important difference: you state, "create" and "manifest" instead of "attract" or "draw." But it is necessary to think about your words in a different way, to have the idea of creation at the basis of all your work. Also, it is important to keep this process in mind even when you are not actually using Words of Power.

CHAPTER TEN

VISUALIZATION

Visualization is a wonderful technique to use along with Words of Power. Everybody has a personal style of visualization. Try to develop your own. Here are some suggestions.

HOW TO VISUALIZE

1. State your Words of Power with your goal—then:

2. Sit or lie comfortably.

3. Close your eyes.

4. Breathe deeply and evenly.

5. Relax your body.

6. Relax your mind; think of this process as easy and natural.

7. Affirm that this work will be pleasant.

8. Allow a picture to come before your eyes, very much like on a giant movie screen, or

9. Allow a scene to appear and surround you. In this case, you are now *in the picture.*

When visualizing something for yourself, it is usually best to be in the picture, because the goal is something that you desire to experience personally. It's more effective to put yourself into the scene by picturing the scene all around you.

Try to experience your visualizations as if you were living them, in a way that is realistic and complete. This way, you not only observe what is in the picture, you also hear it, smell it, and feel it with your senses. Place as many details in each picture as you can.

When you say your Words of Power Statement, it is part of your visualization. As mentioned above, the beginning is a good time to make your statement. Remember, you are the director of your own visualization as well as the principal actor. Therefore, you should try to picture everything as perfectly you want it to be—even if at first this seems impossible. You may wish to use the phrase, *"This, its equivalent, or better (EQOB)"* in reference to your goal. You may wish to say your Words of Power Statement at the end of your visualization, instead of at the beginning. It's up to you.

WHAT NOT TO VISUALIZE

Never visualize *negative images:* If negative images do happen to come into your mind, this is an indication to do some Words of Power work to change the negative into the positive forms you want.

Never visualize *manipulation* of others, ever! Manipulation is often a misunderstanding of magical work, and causes negative results.

There may be an *emotional component* in your visualization. If you feel worried, frightened or otherwise in the grips of a limiting emotion, this could affect the results. The best technique here is, not to deny the problem, but to acknowledge it and transform it. Say Words of Power to release any emotional problem and replace it with the goals of your visualization.

For example:

"... I hereby release all doubt, worry, disbelief, fear or any other block to the perfect manifestation of my goal, and I now replace all that with the Infinity of Solution and (re-state goal)..."

Then repeat your the visualization with the desired effect included in it.

Even non-sighted people can do a version of effective visualization by experiencing the goal for themselves, in whatever way feels powerful and comfortable—smell, touch, vibrations, etc.

Remember, *visualization is perception,* and perception is always up to you.

CHAPTER ELEVEN

FEEL-O-VISION

That's what I call it—the directed use of human emotion to achieve the manifestation of a goal. Actually, at the time of this writing, this technique doesn't yet have a recognized name in our culture, although it is acknowledged as a technique in some popular forms of Affinity Manifestation. I believe that this is a truly ancient technique, because it provides a missing link, an adjunct to visualization, ritual and Words of Power. This is a controlled application of human emotion which I suppose was automatically built into every magical process, long ago. I confess I made up this name to apply to manifestation, based on experiments for phenomena that were meant to transform entertainment when I was a child: smell-o-vision, 3-D movies, and yes, feel-o-vision. Unfortunately, most of these devices fizzled out. They were grand ideas with silly results. Smell-o-vision featured scratch and sniff cards that were meant to illustrate turning points in the plot. The actors would walk through a field of flowers, and you scratched the first spot on the card and sniffed the flowers, then they sat in front of a fireplace and you scratched the next spot and sniffed that smoke. It was a novel idea, but doomed. As for 3-D movies, everyone in the audience had to wear special cardboard glasses, and they basically didn't work. Now, every few years, someone tries to resurrect that cardboard technology, which still hasn't worked adequately. And Feel-O-Vision: that had to do with the seats! The seats moved and jiggled and provided other sensations in a vain attempt to match the action on screen. Actually, this technique is being revived as we speak, and the more expensive the equipment, the better it works—under various new names. But the name Feel-o-vision stuck with me, and now we have a new and effective use for it: the directed use of our own feelings as a source of power—or *feeling plus visualization.*

Usually, our feelings seem autonomous, as if they have a life all their own. They may seem to be mostly reactions to events, people and other stimuli. Often our feelings are powerful; sometimes they can seem to overwhelm us. If our feelings are negative—such as anger, frustration or depression—we may struggle with them because we don't want them to "take over." This is perception. If our feelings are positive—happy, excited or inspired—they still seem to exist in response to something that "made" us feel that way. We may seek whatever it was that seemed to "give" us that feeling: exercise, religion, food, sex, romance or drugs. What we often do not realize, is that *we gave ourselves the feelings*—all of them. The illusion is that it seems as if events or people or whatever stimuli came along created our feelings.

But get this: *Our feelings created the events!* They created the interactions with people—actually the people themselves! Or at least their presence in our lives. Our feelings *create.* So here is this vast, untapped source of power. Or is it an impediment to the use of our personal power? Unfortunately, it often can serve to be an impediment. For example, how can someone work Words of Power for success in some endeavor, if feeling discouraged? Or how can one work for self-healing if feeling sick, or work for happiness if feeling depressed, or work for abundance if feeling a sense of lack? Well, with Words of Power, we can label the negative feeling, release it, and then replace it with the desired goal. But to actually replace the feeling itself with a more positive and appropriate feeling is often a speedier and more effective technique. The reason? *The feeling creates a corresponding image of itself.*

To be simplistic: A happy feeling creates happy circumstances. A wealthy feeling creates wealth and abundance. A feeling of loss can create further loss in other areas. This is the reason that when a person experiences the death of a loved one, other losses often occur in the World of Form: loss of money, of friendships or of material belongings. And if a person feels depressed, sad things just "seem" to happen. It really isn't quite so simple, because other factors are at play, such as karmic ones. For example, a person could be feeling depressed and lonely, and suddenly friends and loved ones could come along and provide comfort to transform that negative feeling. However, usually if one feels depressed and lonely, one would find oneself increasingly alone and surrounded by sad circumstances—unless and until that person does something to change the pattern. The pattern can always be changed, because we created it in the first place.

Sometimes one creates a change that appears to come from outside the self (such as the previously mentioned friends). But, according to this worldview, all changes come from within the self. The idea that outside events cause anything at all in our lives, is an illusion. *We cause the event.* And surprisingly often, we cause the event by means of our feelings. The event echoes and demonstrates our feelings, just as it demonstrates our beliefs and ideas.

USING YOUR FEELINGS

Feelings can be effective tools. Here's how to use them:

1. First of all, be aware of what feelings create: *actual circumstances* in our lives.

2. Next, be aware that you can control and direct your feelings. The easiest way to use them is to *feel* the way you believe you would feel, the way you really want to feel, after your goal has already been accomplished— that is, the goal of your Words of Power work. In other words, experience and feel the fulfillment of your goal, even before it manifests in the World of Form.

Sometimes it may seem difficult or even impossible to create a feeling before you actually experience the goal. Sometimes you might even experience a negative feeling that seems like it won't budge—or a negative feeling that goes away, and then seems to bounce right back again. The antidote: with a Words Of Power Statement, release the negative feeling and replace it with your feeling of choice. Use the positive feeling you want as a goal after you release the negative one. But what if even that seems difficult?

There are techniques for mastering your feelings, so that they become available for your use. Of course, this is does not mean in any way to hide or submerge your true feelings. These techniques are to be used after you acknowledge your feelings, honor them, and then choose to release their grip on your future progress.

DEALING WITH FEELINGS THAT SEEM DIFFICULT

1. Acknowledge and *experience* the unwanted feeling for as long or as short a time as seems minimally necessary, and

2. then completely turn your attention to something else. Think about a number of pleasant things, until you choose one that makes you feel generally good. If there are several effective ideas, make a list and use them as needed.

The point is to switch over to feeling back in control, comfortable, and happy. This should be your starting point for the work, because this is approximately how you want your goal to feel. It really doesn't matter what the subject is; the *feeling* is what matters. So if I feel worried or afraid of something, I acknowledge that for just long enough to know what it feels like, and then I switch over to thinking about my little dogs and how good their silly cavorting makes me feel.

Well, that's what works for me. I know that at first glance this could be interpreted as superficial or naive. But who cares! This is a technique that actually works, doesn't hurt, and always helps. Instead of dogs, you could use a Mozart opera, a Tchaikovsky ballet, a popular song (old or new), the Gettysburg Address or anything else that reliably makes you feel good. One technique is to select one positive attribute of yourself, and name and perceive that. Another technique is to focus on a different positive attribute of yourself each day—for a month! That would amount to approximately thirty positive attributes. These are all tools to enhance the effectiveness of your words.

This process of switching the subject matter closely resembles sense-memory techniques used by actors. A famous actress once disclosed that when she needed tears for a tragic scene, she thought about her dog dying, and her tears were convincing and genuinely wet, because they were real. Well, my technique works the same way—except in this case, my dogs are healthy and happy.

FOR FULL-TIME CONTROL OF FEELINGS

Just as we do well to watch our words even when we are off-duty from working Words of Power, just as we control negative statements by taking them out of the Law (of Cause and Effect) or adding, "No harmful power; turn this to good"—so can we watch our feelings and control them as well.

In the story of Peter Pan, Wendy and her siblings are instructed by Peter—who can fly—to "think lovely thoughts." This is his secret technique. "Picnics... candy... Christmas...!" they gleefully announce. And then they are aloft.7

SPECIFIC FEELINGS

Another effective technique is to relive an occasion that made you feel specifically the way you want your goal to make you feel. If you are using Words of Power for abundance, relive the way you felt when you got your first allowance, or your first job, if these are appropriate examples. Otherwise, of course pick another one. If you are doing Words of Power for yourself healing, feel the way you felt at your most athletic and strong. If your goal is love, feel the way you felt when you were the most loved, even if that love was in your childhood, from your mother—or from your dog! It doesn't matter what you use as your sense memory to relive your feeling. Just get the feeling, harness it, and send it out along with your Words. If you think that the feeling source is inappropriate for your current goal—even though its intensity and vibration is correct—you can always add an adjustment to your Words of Power: "I now feel as loved as I did the first time Spot licked my face, only this time, the feeling comes from a human love relationship, licking not entirely necessary."

Just be careful when you choose to work with a sense memory feeling: when you wish to relive something, only relive that which is positive. If other problems seem to be mixed in with the memory, let that particular memory go, and choose something else.

EXPANDED GOALS

People who advocate working for manifestation with feelings are generally devoted to the Infinity of Solution—even if not by that name. Because limitation is a feeling, they encourage their students to seek and feel *unlimited goals.* Such goals are sometimes not even named. Only you will know if this is an appropriate technique for you.

Feel-o-vision—or whatever we choose to call it—may seem difficult to use at first, but it is not really difficult, just different. It presents an entirely new context for dealing with life. As we practice it, we can grow more comfortable with working in this way, and the results will help us to transcend any initial disbelief. I suspect that time will reveal infinite possibilities in working with the power of feelings.

I have also researched, written and talked about a related subject I call *Personal Magic, The Role and the True Self.*[8] An awareness of the True Self is an enlightening source of self-awareness and fulfillment, which also happens to be a way to deepen the effectiveness of Words of Power. When I began researching Words of Power all those years ago, I didn't even know about the concept of the True Self. Now that I do, I suspect that all the experiences and information we encounter in our lives inevitably contribute to our manifestation work. Bringing in The True Self is a wonderful way to add power and strength to Words of Power. The Role and The True Self is a big subject, but for our purposes here, we can simply use it as awareness.

The True Self is that deepest and most authentic part of each one of us that most directly accesses the link we all have to the Universal Power Source. On the other hand, the *Role* is a method most of us have used, in varying degrees, to "pass" or fit in. In this culture, The Role comes from childhood, when it served as a coping mechanism. Sadly, many of us continue playing some version of The Role throughout adulthood also. When we work Words of Power out of a feeling of playing a Role, the work can often be delayed and confused. We may not even choose a goal correctly according to our true needs. Try to choose your goals and work your Words of Power Statements directly out of your True Self, not from the vantage point of any Roles.

COMPOSING YOUR OWN WORDS OF POWER STATEMENT

Since I wrote my first sentence about Words of Power, and all my subsequent development of this subject over the years—I have repeatedly recommended that you write your own original Words of Power Statements.

I have provided instructions, outlines, background and tons of relevant information. But I kept insisting, "Never, *never,* NEVER repeat Words of Power (or chants or affirmations or anything else) that someone else has written or provided for you. Never!"

But you *can* teach an old Witch new tricks! With my website, *www.marionweinstein.com* and my Words of Power web page, and the help of a couple of local geniuses—I realized that I can provide Words of Power Statements for people and still let them be personal. I can do this by giving the components. I can also provide the Statement's basic outline—with, of course, a complete explanation (that would be this book). You can then choose from variations for each area of your Words of Power Statement. And you can personalize your Statement with each choice.

You can choose from the following components:

- Your goal

- Your style

- Your Power Source

- Your relationship to your Power Source

- Your manifestation of your goal as automatic

- remember "According to Free Will and For The Good of All"

- Your release—which means everything you want to get rid of

- Your repeated manifestation of your goal

- Your finale style: How to end your Statement and send it off into the Universe.

Following this outline, the Statement would be karmically correct, powerful—and personal.

Of course you can compose your Words of Power Statement without using any of these components as provided here. However, I do strongly recommend that you follow the basic outline.

If you insist, you can even change the *sequence* of steps, as long as you include all the steps, and know why you are including them.

Otherwise, your Statement might be a wonderful affirmation or prayer—but it would not be Words of Power. This, of course, is fine. However, *these instructions are for Words of Power.*

Chapter Twelve

The Components And The Sequence: General Outline For A Words Of Power Statement

1. Choose a name for your Power Source

2. Define your goal(s) as part of the Universal Power

3. Name and align yourself as a perfect incarnation of the Universal Power

4. State that your goal(s) will manifest—with your participation

5. According to free will

6. And for the good of all

7. Release negatives

8. Replace them with life-affirming positives; reaffirm your goal

9. Pick a finale style—which will send your Statement out into the Universe

Note: In this work, the Words of Power Statement is the cause, and the manifestation is the effect—when your words "come true."

WORDS OF POWER STATEMENT FOR THE GOAL OF LOVE

Generic Style:

1. There is One Power, which is The Universal Power

2. Which includes perfect love of every kind

3. And I (your name here) am The Universal Power incarnate

4. Therefore I create and manifest perfect love in my life here, now and always

5. According to free will

6. And for the good of all

7. I now release all cause, effect, manifestation, form and essence, belief or idea anything less than perfect love

8. I replace this with perfect love of every kind, here, now, and always

9. And so this must be!

Note: A variation on step 4 above— "Therefore I create and manifest *myself as perfect love* in my life here, now and always."

SUGGESTED GOALS FOR YOU TO CHOOSE

- Health
- Love
- Safety/Protection
- Wealth
- Balance
- Comfort
- Home
- Peace
- Success
- Clarity
- Spirituality
- Relationships
- Fulfillment
- Confidence
- Joy
- Psychic Power/Intuition
- Creativity
- Peace/Serenity

CHOOSE A POWER SOURCE

- God
- Goddess
- God & Goddess
- Goddess & God
- God Force
- Goddess Force
- Great Spirit
- Higher Power
- Lord & Lady
- Nature
- Universal Life Force
- Universal Power

FINALE STYLES

- Generic — So This Must Be!
- Judeo Christian — Amen!
- Outer Space — Make It So!
- Pagan — So Mote It Be!
- Positive Magic/Wiccan — So Mote It Be!
- Scientific — I Now Release This Into The Law Of Cause And Effect!
- Tribal/Native — And So It Is!

ADDITIONAL POWER SOURCES

DEITIES[9]

If you wish to work in greater detail, Goddesses and Gods from other lands and earlier times are all sacred. They are still available to us today for inspiration and sources of personal power. Here are just a few examples of the rich array of Deities for you to contemplate, research and choose from.

GODDESSES

- **DIANA** (*Roman*)—Goddess of the Hunt, protector of children and animals. Rules the Waxing Moon and New Beginnings.

- **SELENE** (*Greek*)—Goddess of The Full Moon and infinite possibilities.

- **HECATE** (*Turkish and Greek*), *Hekate*—Goddess of The Waning and Dark Moon, rules justice and clarity. Rules the crossroads and choices.

- **KERNUNNOS** (*Celtic*), *Cernunnos*—God of The Hunt, the hearth, positive sexual energy, love and dance.

- **PAN** (*Greek and Roman and throughout Europe*)—
God of the Woodlands and mountains. Delights in
nature, sometimes depicted as goat-footed, playing his
musical pipes, He rules entertainment and merriment.

- **ARTEMIS** (*Greek*)—Goddess of healing, the Moon,
wild animals, and physical strength in women. The
twin of Apollo. Greek version of *Diana*.

- **CERES** (*Roman*)—Goddess of the grain, the harvest,
and the Earth. Founder of the legal system, the Great
Mother Nurturer. Women pray to Her when they want
to have children.

- **HESTIA** (*Greek*)— First of all Divinities to be involved
in all prayers. Essentially the same Goddess as Vesta.
(*Roman*)—Goddess of the hearth and safe spaces. Her
altar was the most sacred space in Rome and Her flame
never went out. Her priestesses were called Vestal
Virgins. At the time, virginity meant independence, not
chastity.

- **ATHENA** (*Greek*)—Goddess of wisdom, Warrior
Goddess. Her temple was the Parthenon.

- **YEMENYA** (*African*) Alternate spellings: *Yemaya,
Inmanja*—Originally from Africa, but also later
Brazilian. Holy Queen of the Sea. Has Dominion over
the Summer Solstice, and protects boats.

- **MORRIGAN** (*Celtic*)—A Triple Goddess. Mainly
referred to as *"The Morrigan."* Courageous, shapeshift-
er, sometimes associated with the other world (after
death).

- **GAIA** (*Greek*)—Mother Nature. The Goddess of the

planet Earth. Now Her name has come up again in the environmental movement, to tell us that the Earth is sacred and that we are all part of one Being.

- **ISIS** (*Egyptian*)—Also known as *Hathor Isis,* Her milk was believed to have created the Milky Way. She ruled invention, law, agriculture, healing—and was known for miracles and magic words. I have based my work on Her *Words of Power.*

- **NUT** (*Egyptian*)—Sky Goddess, ruler of the night, the subconscious (dreams), and the stars.

- **JUNO** (*Roman*)—Queen of Heaven, Mother of The Goddesses and Gods, numerous other titles. She ruled most areas of life and watched over all women.

- **HERA** (*Greek name of Juno*).

- **DEVI** (*East Indian*)—An all-encompassing Indian Goddess, She was said to hold the Guna strands of existence that make us see things as so-called "reality." This has a modern counterpart in atomic particles.

- **IX CHEL** (*Mexican*)—Goddess of birth and the Moon.

- **ISHTAR** (*Near Eastern*)—Goddess of love, of prophetic visions, oracles, and prophecy; Goddess of all nourishment; Her most famous title, "Queen of Heaven," was one of many praise-filled titles.

- **RHIANNON** (*Celtic*)—Goddess of the Other World. Birds are sacred to Her, specifically the raven.

- **CERRIDWEN** (Celtic)—Goddess of the Cauldron, birth and rebirth. The Birch is Her sacred tree.

- **AWEHAL** (*Iroquois*)—Goddess who created the Earth, seeds and animals.

- **MAWU** (*Native American*)—She is said to have put a little piece of Herself (Sekpoli) in each person.

- **NAMMU/NINA** (*Near Eastern*)—The oldest Goddess name in recorded history. The Mother of all Deities.

- **SPIDER WOMAN** (*Native American*)—The Creatrix of the peoples of the Desert Circle: Southwest United States and North Mexico, She wove existence—all the world—out of the Sun's rays. Also called *Spider Grandmother.*

- **GUADELUPE** (*Mexican, Aztec*)—A Brown Goddess and still a principal Deity in Mexico, She stands between the Moon and Sun's rays; Her cloak is covered with stars. In the 16th Century, She became the "Patron Saint of the Western Hemisphere."

- **OYA** (*African, Yoruba*)—Ruler of wind, fire and thunder—and female power. The female Warrior Goddess, also healer and transformer.

GODS

- **OSIRIS** (*Egyptian*)—Consort/Husband to Isis. Rules the underworld and redefines death. Known for His miraculous regenerative capabilities. His symbol is the ankh:

- **NEPTUNE** (*Roman*)—God of the sea, ruler of dreams and visions. The planet Neptune is named after Him.

- **POSEIDON** (*Greek*)—Aspect of Neptune (see above).

- **APOLLO** (*Greek*)—Twin to Artemis. God of the Sun, music and medicine.

- **HERMES** (*Greek*), Mercury (*Roman*)—Messenger God. Rules communication.

- **HORUS** (*Egyptian*)—God of the living, sacred child of Isis and Osiris. His symbol, *The Eye Of Horus,* represents life within death.

- **RA** (*Egyptian*)—Sun God, parent of all the Gods and Goddesses.

- **CHAC NOH EK** (*Mexican*)—Brother/Lover of the Sun star Venus. Sky God.

- **TAMMUZ** (*Near Eastern*)—Consort of Ishtar. God of the Harvest, agriculture and love.

- **ESHU** (*African, Yoruba*)—Also known as Legba and Baba (Father), guardian of homes and villages. Trickster, protector, teacher, rules literacy and divination of the future.

- **OBATALA** (*African, Yoruba*)—Father, Creator. He represents clarity, justice and wisdom, with dominion over hell, peace, and harmony. Also, ruler of everything that is white on Earth (snow, bones, etc.). Sometimes *seen as androgynous*—both male and female.

WORKING WITH GODDESSES AND GODS

These are just some of the Gods and Goddesses available for you to use as Power Sources.

Choose the qualities most meaningful to you, and know that they change over time. You can choose different Deities for different Words of Power Statements.

Words of Power Statement Using Goddess and God For The Goal Of Fulfillment

Generic Style

1. There is One Power

2. Which is Goddess and God

3. Which includes perfect fulfillment

4. And I (your name here) am Goddess Incarnate

5. Perfectly aligned with God

   Or:

   I am God Incarnate

   Perfectly aligned with Goddess

6. Therefore I create and manifest perfect fulfillment in my life here and now

7. According to free will

8. And for the good of all

9. I release all cause, effect, manifestation, form and essence of anything less than perfect fulfillment in my life

10. Therefore perfect fulfillment is mine, here and now

11. And so this must be!

Instead of saying "God" or "Goddess" as above, you may insert actual names, for example: "I am Isis incarnate, perfectly aligned with Osiris" or "I am Tammuz incarnate, perfectly aligned with Ishtar." Or any of the above names in combination.

QUALIFIERS

You may wish to add one or more of these phrases at the end of your Words of Power Statement:

- With joy and with ease

- With perfect timing and spacing

- With reinforcement for encouragement

- From my True Self to my True Self

The place to add one or more of these qualifiers is just *before* the finale line.

USING WORDS OF POWER TO HELP OTHER PEOPLE

Ideally, everyone should compose and say his/her own Words of Power Statements. You can write a Statement for another person and give it to that person to say, but *you* should not say it for anyone else unless they give you permission—because that would be:

a. Manipulative

b. Denying the other's personal power

EXCEPTIONS

What about healing? Sometimes we can't get the other's permission because the person might be too sick to speak. In such a case, we can say a Words of Power Statement for the other, remembering the vital components of *According to free will, and For the good of all.* One good goal when working for another is: "All (name's) needs and wants fulfilled." If any use of Words of Power is not karmically appropriate, the Statement simply will not go out into the Universe.

A related point:

We cannot say who should win and who should lose—anything, from a ball game to an election to a war.

GROUP WORK

We can work in a group, taking turns.

We can do "back-up" for another, only when asked. And of course we can ask another to do back-up for us.

Working For Multiple Goals

In my circle, some of us often work for a multiplicity of goals within one Words of Power Statement. This can be confusing, and is not recommended here unless you have reason to believe you absolutely must do so. Usually a sequence of single Statements is clearer.

Words of Power Statement for The Multiple Goals Of Health, Abundance and love

Generic Style

1. There is One Power

2. Which is health, abundance and love

3. And I (your name here)

4. Am a perfect manifestation of the One Power

5. Therefore perfect health, abundance and love are mine

6. According to free will

7. And for the good of all

8. I release all illness, all lack and all loneliness

9. And I manifest in my life perfect health, abundance and love

10. And so this must be!

Preliminary Statements

If You Are Unsure Of Your Goal

Simply work a preliminary Words of Power Statement with the goal of "choosing my perfect goal." Then work a second Statement with that goal.

If You Don't Feel Ready

You may work a preliminary Words of Power Statement with the goal of "readiness to work Words of Power for my goal." Then work a second Words of Power Statement for your goal.

Timing

How often to say your Words of Power Statement? At least once, and preferably once a day or once every few days. In between these times, when you think about your Words of Power Statement, you may refer to it like this:

1. *My Statement is working. (Insert any finale style)*

   Or

2. *The spell is working. And So Mote It Be.*

3. (If doubts crop up) *No harmful power; turn this to good.*

Or you may use one of these shortcuts:

SHORTCUTS

1. The one Power working for me and through me creates and manifests (state goal)...

2. The Goddess and God (name any Power Source) working for me and through me (your name) create and manifest (state goal)...

3. Everything I need to know, I know
Everything I need to do, I do
Everything I need to have, I have
According to Free Will and For the Good of all
With (state Power Source) working for me and through me
I release (state release)
And create all that I know, do and have.

(Choose a finale style for any of the above variations & shortcuts)

Afterword

Words create our worlds and transform reality. We are constantly creating and transforming our realities, even if we are unaware that we are doing this. When we make the choice to use Words of Power in a deliberate, thoughtful and informed way, our manifestations are most effective and safe.

"Come to me, for my speech hath in it the power to protect, and it possesseth life... For I am Isis the Goddess, and I am the Lady of Words of Power, and I know how to work with Words of Power, and most mighty are my words!"

Remember this message from Isis.

Remember—Most mighty are *your* Words!

NOTES

1. Budge, E.A. Wallis, trans., *The Gods of the Egyptians,* Part 1 & 2, Kessinger Publishing, LLC, 2003

2. Bergier, Jacques, and Pauwels, Louis, *The Morning Of The Magicians,* Souvenir Press; New edition 2007

3. John 1:1

4. Acts 7:22

5. *The I Ching,* hexagram #37. Wilhelm/Baynes translation, Princeton, N.J., Bollingen Series, Princeton University Press, 1970.

6. Ellen Goldman Shapiro invented the term "EQOB" as a short version of "This, its equivalent or better."

7. *Peter Pan.* Lyrics by Caroline Leigh, Music by Mark Charlap, additional lyrics by Betty Comden and Adolph Green, additional music by Jule Styne, Hal Leanard Corporation.

8. *Personal Magic; The Role And The True Self.* CD and audiotape, written and hosted by Marion Weinstein, Produced by Earth Magic Productions, Inc. NY. 1998. (Soon to be a book).

9. Weinstein, Marion. *Earth Magic; A Guide for Positive Witches,* Franklin Lakes, New Jersey. New Page Books, Career Press, Inc. 2003

10. *Magic For Peace, A Nonsectarian Guide to Working Positive Magic for Peace and Safety,* by Marion Weinstein, Earth Magic Productions, Inc. NY 2007.

11. △⁎̣ Symbol of Isis in the heavens as the beloved star Sept.

△⃰ △⃰ △⃰

WORDS OF POWER STATEMENT OUTLINES

Personalized Interactive Words Of Power Statements can be found at www.marionweinstein.com.

THE GODDESS ISIS

Words of Power Statement for the goal of_____
Goal

for_____
Your Name

1. There is One Power, which is _____
Power Source

2. Which includes perfect _____ of every
   kind   Goal

3. And I, _____, am _____
   incarnate   Your Name   Power Source

4. Therefore I manifest perfect _____in my
   life here, now and always   Goal

5. For the good of all

6. According to free will

7. I now release all cause, effect, manifestation, form, essence, belief
   or anything less than complete _____
   Goal

8. I replace this with perfect _____of every
   kind, here, now, and always   Goal

9. _____!
   Finale Style

Words of Power Statement for the goal of_____
Goal

for_____
Your Name

1. There is One Power, which is _____
Power Source

2. Which includes perfect _____ of every
kind   Goal

3. And I, _____, am _____
incarnate   Your Name   Power Source

4. Therefore I manifest perfect _____ in my
life here, now and always   Goal

5. For the good of all

6. According to free will

7. I now release all cause, effect, manifestation, form, essence, belief
or anything less than complete _____
Goal

8. I replace this with perfect _____ of every
kind, here, now, and always   Goal

9. _____!
Finale Style

Words of Power Statement for the goal of_____
Goal

for_____
Your Name

1. There is One Power, which is _____
Power Source

2. Which includes perfect _____ of every
kind
Goal

3. And I, _____, am _____
incarnate   Your Name   Power Source

4. Therefore I manifest perfect _____in my
life here, now and always
Goal

5. For the good of all

6. According to free will

7. I now release all cause, effect, manifestation, form, essence, belief
or anything less than complete _____
Goal

8. I replace this with perfect _____of every
kind, here, now, and always
Goal

9. _____!
Finale Style

Words of Power Statement for the goal of_____
Goal

for_____
Your Name

1. There is One Power, which is _____
Power Source

2. Which includes perfect _____ of every
kind
Goal

3. And I, _____, am _____
incarnate
Your Name   Power Source

4. Therefore I manifest perfect _____in my
life here, now and always
Goal

5. For the good of all

6. According to free will

7. I now release all cause, effect, manifestation, form, essence, belief
or anything less than complete _____
Goal

8. I replace this with perfect _____of every
kind, here, now, and always
Goal

9. _____!
Finale Style

Words of Power Statement for the goal of_____
Goal

for_____
Your Name

1. There is One Power, which is _____
Power Source

2. Which includes perfect _____ of every
   kind
Goal

3. And I,_____, am _____
   incarnate   Your Name   Power Source

4. Therefore I manifest perfect _____in my
   life here, now and always   Goal

5. For the good of all

6. According to free will

7. I now release all cause, effect, manifestation, form, essence, belief
   or anything less than complete _____
Goal

8. I replace this with perfect _____of every
   kind, here, now, and always   Goal

9. _____ !
Finale Style

Words of Power Statement for the goal of_____
                                                    Goal

        for_____
                        Your Name

1. There is One Power, which is _____
                                        Power Source

2. Which includes perfect _____ of every
   kind   Goal

3. And I, _____, am _____
   incarnate   Your Name   Power Source

4. Therefore I manifest perfect _____in my
                                            Goal
   life here, now and always

5. For the good of all

6. According to free will

7. I now release all cause, effect, manifestation, form, essence, belief
   or anything less than complete _____
                                            Goal

8. I replace this with perfect _____of every
                                            Goal
   kind, here, now, and always

9. _____!
              Finale Style

Words of Power Statement for the goal of_____
Goal

for_____
Your Name

1. There is One Power, which is _____
Power Source

2. Which includes perfect _____ of every
kind   Goal

3. And I, _____, am _____
incarnate   Your Name   Power Source

4. Therefore I manifest perfect _____in my
life here, now and always   Goal

5. For the good of all

6. According to free will

7. I now release all cause, effect, manifestation, form, essence, belief
or anything less than complete _____
Goal

8. I replace this with perfect _____of every
kind, here, now, and always   Goal

9. _____!
Finale Style

Words of Power Statement for the goal of_____
                                                              Goal

for_____
                          Your Name

1. There is One Power, which is _____
                                                   Power Source

2. Which includes perfect _____ of every
   kind   Goal

3. And I, _____, am _____
   incarnate   Your Name   Power Source

4. Therefore I manifest perfect _____in my
   life here, now and always   Goal

5. For the good of all

6. According to free will

7. I now release all cause, effect, manifestation, form, essence, belief
   or anything less than complete _____
                                                       Goal

8. I replace this with perfect _____of every
   kind, here, now, and always   Goal

9. _____!
                          Finale Style

Words of Power Statement for the goal of_____
Goal

for_____
Your Name

1. There is One Power, which is _____
Power Source

2. Which includes perfect _____ of every
   kind
Goal

3. And I, _____, am _____
   incarnate   Your Name   Power Source

4. Therefore I manifest perfect _____in my
   life here, now and always
Goal

5. For the good of all

6. According to free will

7. I now release all cause, effect, manifestation, form, essence, belief
   or anything less than complete _____
Goal

8. I replace this with perfect _____of every
   kind, here, now, and always
Goal

9. _____!
Finale Style

Words of Power Statement for the goal of_____
                                                    Goal

        for_____
                        Your Name

1. There is One Power, which is _____
                                        Power Source

2. Which includes perfect _____ of every
                                    Goal
   kind

3. And I, _____, am _____
              Your Name   Power Source
   incarnate

4. Therefore I manifest perfect _____in my
                                        Goal
   life here, now and always

5. For the good of all

6. According to free will

7. I now release all cause, effect, manifestation, form, essence, belief
   or anything less than complete _____
                                            Goal

8. I replace this with perfect _____of every
                                        Goal
   kind, here, now, and always

9. _____!
                        Finale Style

Words of Power Statement for the goal of_____
                                           Goal

        for_____
                        Your Name

1. There is One Power, which is _____
                                           Power Source

2. Which includes perfect _____ of every
   kind   Goal

3. And I, _____, am _____
   incarnate   Your Name   Power Source

4. Therefore I manifest perfect _____in my
   life here, now and always   Goal

5. For the good of all

6. According to free will

7. I now release all cause, effect, manifestation, form, essence, belief
   or anything less than complete _____
                                              Goal

8. I replace this with perfect _____of every
   kind, here, now, and always   Goal

9. _____!
                        Finale Style

Words of Power Statement for the goal of_____
Goal

for_____
Your Name

1. There is One Power, which is _____
Power Source

2. Which includes perfect _____ of every
kind
Goal

3. And I, _____, am _____
incarnate
Your Name   Power Source

4. Therefore I manifest perfect _____in my
life here, now and always
Goal

5. For the good of all

6. According to free will

7. I now release all cause, effect, manifestation, form, essence, belief
or anything less than complete _____
Goal

8. I replace this with perfect _____of every
kind, here, now, and always
Goal

9. _____!
Finale Style

Words of Power Statement for the goal of_____
Goal

for_____
Your Name

1. There is One Power, which is _____
Power Source

2. Which includes perfect _____ of every
   kind
Goal

3. And I, _____, am _____
   incarnate   Your Name   Power Source

4. Therefore I manifest perfect _____in my
   life here, now and always
Goal

5. For the good of all

6. According to free will

7. I now release all cause, effect, manifestation, form, essence, belief
   or anything less than complete _____
Goal

8. I replace this with perfect _____of every
   kind, here, now, and always
Goal

9. _____!
Finale Style

Words of Power Statement for the goal of_____
Goal

for_____
Your Name

1. There is One Power, which is _____
Power Source

2. Which includes perfect _____ of every
   kind
Goal

3. And I, _____, am _____
   incarnate
Your Name   Power Source

4. Therefore I manifest perfect _____in my
   life here, now and always
Goal

5. For the good of all

6. According to free will

7. I now release all cause, effect, manifestation, form, essence, belief
   or anything less than complete _____
Goal

8. I replace this with perfect _____of every
   kind, here, now, and always
Goal

9. _____!
Finale Style

Words of Power Statement for the goal of_____
Goal

for_____
Your Name

1. There is One Power, which is _____
Power Source

2. Which includes perfect _____ of every
kind   Goal

3. And I, _____, am _____
incarnate   Your Name   Power Source

4. Therefore I manifest perfect _____in my
life here, now and always   Goal

5. For the good of all

6. According to free will

7. I now release all cause, effect, manifestation, form, essence, belief
or anything less than complete _____
Goal

8. I replace this with perfect _____of every
kind, here, now, and always   Goal

9. _____!
Finale Style

Words of Power Statement for the goal of_____
                                                    Goal

       for_____
                                                    Your Name

1. There is One Power, which is _____
                                                    Power Source

2. Which includes perfect _____ of every
   kind   Goal

3. And I, _____, am _____
                    Your Name   Power Source
   incarnate

4. Therefore I manifest perfect _____in my
                                                    Goal
   life here, now and always

5. For the good of all

6. According to free will

7. I now release all cause, effect, manifestation, form, essence, belief
   or anything less than complete _____
                                                    Goal

8. I replace this with perfect _____of every
                                                    Goal
   kind, here, now, and always

9. _____!
                        Finale Style

Words of Power Statement for the goal of_____
Goal

for_____
Your Name

1. There is One Power, which is _____
Power Source

2. Which includes perfect _____ of every
   kind   Goal

3. And I, _____, am _____
   incarnate   Your Name   Power Source

4. Therefore I manifest perfect _____in my
   life here, now and always   Goal

5. For the good of all

6. According to free will

7. I now release all cause, effect, manifestation, form, essence, belief
   or anything less than complete _____
   Goal

8. I replace this with perfect _____of every
   kind, here, now, and always   Goal

9. _____!
   Finale Style

Words of Power Statement for the goal of_____
Goal

for_____
Your Name

1. There is One Power, which is _____
Power Source

2. Which includes perfect _____ of every
   kind
Goal

3. And I, _____, am _____
   incarnate   Your Name   Power Source

4. Therefore I manifest perfect _____in my
   life here, now and always
Goal

5. For the good of all

6. According to free will

7. I now release all cause, effect, manifestation, form, essence, belief
   or anything less than complete _____.
Goal

8. I replace this with perfect _____of every
   kind, here, now, and always
Goal

9. _____!
Finale Style

Words of Power Statement for the goal of_____
Goal

for_____
Your Name

1. There is One Power, which is _____
Power Source

2. Which includes perfect _____ of every
   kind
Goal

3. And I, _____, am _____
   incarnate   Your Name   Power Source

4. Therefore I manifest perfect _____in my
   life here, now and always
Goal

5. For the good of all

6. According to free will

7. I now release all cause, effect, manifestation, form, essence, belief
   or anything less than complete _____
Goal

8. I replace this with perfect _____of every
   kind, here, now, and always
Goal

9. _____!
Finale Style

Words of Power Statement for the goal of_____
                                                              Goal

for_____
                        Your Name

1. There is One Power, which is _____
                                                    Power Source

2. Which includes perfect _____ of every
   kind   Goal

3. And I, _____, am _____
           Your Name   Power Source
   incarnate

4. Therefore I manifest perfect _____in my
                                                    Goal
   life here, now and always

5. For the good of all

6. According to free will

7. I now release all cause, effect, manifestation, form, essence, belief
   or anything less than complete _____
                                                    Goal

8. I replace this with perfect _____of every
                                                    Goal
   kind, here, now, and always

9. _____!
                        Finale Style

Words of Power Statement for the goal of_____
                                                        Goal

for_____
                    Your Name

1. There is One Power, which is _____
                                                Power Source

2. Which includes perfect _____ of every
   kind   Goal

3. And I, _____, am _____
   incarnate   Your Name   Power Source

4. Therefore I manifest perfect _____in my
   life here, now and always   Goal

5. For the good of all

6. According to free will

7. I now release all cause, effect, manifestation, form, essence, belief
   or anything less than complete _____
                                                Goal

8. I replace this with perfect _____of every
   kind, here, now, and always   Goal

9. _____!
                    Finale Style

Words of Power Statements for Planetary Health

Here are 4 Statements you may work to help our planet, Earth.

Saying these Statements is not instead of action—such as dona-
tions, volunteering, acts of charily and other World of Form help
– but in addition to acting in accordance. Of course, if all you can
manage right now is to work of Words of Power, that is powerful
and effective help.

It is recommended that when you work Words of Power for yourself, you take some time and work at least one Statement for the
planet as well. Yes, every time we work for ourselves, we say ""according to free will and for the good of all" and that does inevitably
affect the greater good This is not to be minimized, but specific
Words of Power for our home planet is always helpful,.

Working Words of Power in a group for such a mutual goal is traditionally strong.

The Statements that follow may be subject to variations, as you see
fit.

The Name of The Earth Goddess Gaia may be substituted as the
One Power.

WORDS OF POWER STATEMENT FOR PEACE AND SAFETY IN THE WORLD[10]

Generic Style

1. There is One Universal Power

2. Which is perfect peace and perfect safety

3. And I (your name here) am The One Universal Power incarnate

4. The Universal Power works for and through me, and whoever else wishes to be part of this work, to manifest perfect peace and safety in the world

5. According to free will

6. And for the good of all

7. I now release all cause, effect, manifestation, form and essence, belief or idea of anything less than perfect peace and safety in the world

8. Instead, The Infinity of Solution works perfectly to manifest perfect peace and safety for all.

9. And So This Must Be!

Words of Power Statement for The Goals of Nourishment and Abundance for All

Generic Style

1. There is One Universal Power

2. Which is perfect nourishment and abundance for all

3. And I (your name here) am The One Universal Power Incarnate

4. The Universal Power works for me and through me and whoever else wishes to be part of this work, to manifest perfect nourishment and abundance for all beings in the world

5. According to free will

6. And for the good of all

7. I now release all cause, effect, manifestation, form, essence and belief of anything less than complete nourishment and abundance for all

8. The Infinity of Solution works perfectly to manifest perfect nourishment and abundance for all beings on the Planet Earth

9. And So This Must Be!